Diary of a Dumpster

Diary of a Dumpster Pup

Beverly Keil

Diary of a Dumpster Pup

ISBN-10:1495280640
ISBN-13:978-1495280641

For Becky and the dedicated staff of Pet Network Humane Society, and for my friends Diane, Toni and Cathy who embarked on this rescue mission with me. Thank you also to Heidi, Steve and all the other volunteers who participated in foster care for the Dumpster pups.

Most especially, this book is for all the people who have ever invited an innocent abandoned animal into their homes and into their hearts.

Most of the photos in this book were taken by me using a Smartphone, never expecting to publish a book. Some of the better photos were taken by Becky at Pet Network and the studio quality photos at the end of the book are by Rich Chew, a true artist. Thank you everyone for your permission to publish them.

Thank you also to the North Lake Tahoe Bonanza for following the story of the Dumpster puppies as it unfolded and for publishing weekly abbreviated episodes of my diary.

All proceeds from sales of this book are donated to Pet Network Humane Society.

Pet Network rescues abandoned dogs and cats that face certain euthanasia in overcrowded public shelters. The animals receive medical care and spay or neuter surgeries, and then are placed in new forever homes.

Visit on line at www.petnetwork.org and join us on Facebook at Pet Network Humane Society.

Diary of a Dumpster Pup

Hi.

I am one lucky dog.

But my life didn't start out that way.

Hours after I was born, I was found abandoned in a Dumpster.

My name is Bandit and this is my true story.

Hello.

Bandit doesn't know how lucky he really is.

I took Bandit into my home when he was only hours old.

I became his foster mom and I saved his life.

My name is Beverly and I will help Bandit tell his true story.

Day One
Rescue

Bandit:

What's happening to me? Where is my mom?

I was born a short time ago and left in a Dumpster with my nine brothers and sisters.

My eyes are not yet open. Perhaps that is for the better. I smell nothing good.

I am very hungry and very cold. I need help. There is nothing I can do but cry.

How could anyone leave a litter of newborn puppies in a Dumpster like this?

Oh, something is happening. I am being picked up and moved. I feel a little bit warmer now but I am still hungry. And I am so tired.

Again I am being picked up and moved. I think I am with one of my sisters. Oh, that's nice. I am being wrapped in a blanket. It feels so good to be warm.

Something is pushing at my mouth. Is that Mom? I feel some milk drops in my mouth but I am so tired I can barely swallow. Someone is squeezing milk deeper into my mouth. I try to drink it. But I fall asleep while trying.

I am awakened again and more milk is squeezed into my mouth. This time I try harder. It tastes good and makes me feel better. All I want to do is drink milk and sleep next to my sister on the warm blanket.

Beverly:

I have always loved animals. Since I retired and moved to Lake Tahoe, I have volunteered at the local animal shelter, Pet Network Humane Society.

I am just finishing a Pet Network board meeting when I learn that ten newborn puppies have been found in a Dumpster in South Lake Tahoe, about 30 miles away. A Good Samaritan is bringing the litter to the shelter. Volunteers are needed to foster the pups and try to save their lives.

I have four cats at home. I have never owned nor cared for a dog. But this is an emergency and I wonder: can I do this?

Ten newborn puppies are found abandoned in a Dumpster and brought to the Pet Network shelter.

Thirty minutes later I leave the shelter with a small cat carrier containing two weak newborn pups, a container of powder formula, syringes, bedding, a heating pad and a baby bottle the size of one I had for my dolls when I was six years old.

I received a few quick instructions: keep them warm, warm, warm, feed them every two hours all day and all night, rub their lower tummies to get them to pee and poop after eating. They do not yet have the muscle strength to do this on their own.

And, a reality check: *even if you do everything right, the puppies still may not make it.* In fact, there is only a small chance any of them will survive without their mother. There is no way to know how long they have been abandoned and what they have been exposed to in the Dumpster.

I am home about five minutes when my dinner guests arrive. My husband is cooking. I am inspecting my puppies and bracing for the task ahead. My friend Linda sees the carrier and thinks I have adopted another special needs cat. She is floored to see the puppies. I hand her the brown one and I hold the black one. They look like little rats.

The first bottle feeding for the newborn puppy is challenging.

I mix the formula and warm the bottle. We take turns trying to nurse the pups whose eyes are closed and who still have umbilical cords attached to their tummies. I know they haven't eaten and I think they should devour the milk, but they are so young they don't know how to suckle. We have to force the nipple into their mouths again and again. We also use a syringe from time to time to deliver some of the formula deeper into their mouths.

The black pup seems finally to catch on but we are having trouble getting the brown one to nurse.

The puppies are clearly worn out from the exertion and we place them in their carrier to sleep. They have eaten so little, yet because they are so tiny, I am hoping it may be enough. I set a timer for two hours. We have a glass of wine to ease the stress.

The feeding challenge goes on every two hours and the amount the puppies consume seems miniscule.

The phone keeps ringing. My friends Diane, Toni and Cathy have their own pups and are asking questions. We compare experiences. Are yours sucking the nipple? Did you have to use the syringe? Are yours real wiggly? Have they made any sounds? How much of the formula did you get them to eat? We are all novices at this rescue effort.

Becky from Pet Network also calls to see how we are doing and to provide encouragement. It takes a Village.

My guests leave, thanking us for a great dinner and a very unusual evening. My husband and I stay up all night caring for the pups. I constantly check on their temperature to be sure they are warm enough. They have a heating pad inside their carrier and they sleep together in a corner. Every two hours I carefully mix the formula and warm the bottle. They take turns drinking a little bit at a time.

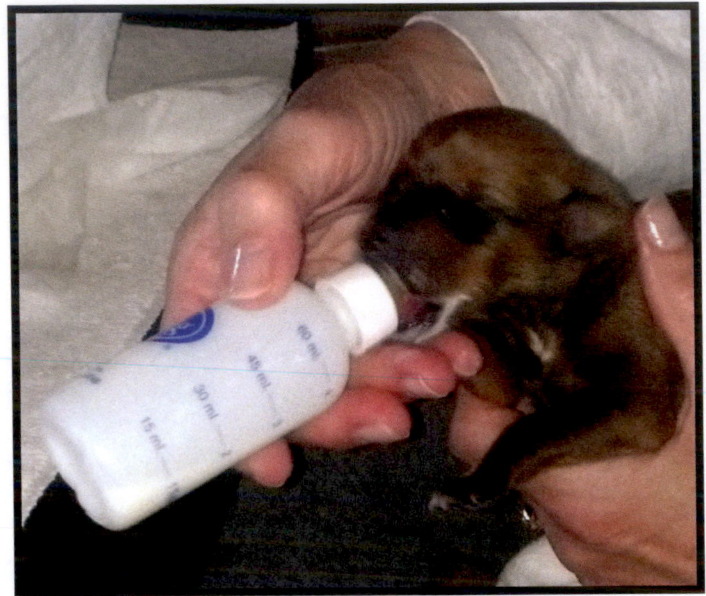

Bottle feeding continues every two hours all day and night.

My puppies make it through the first night, a very important milestone. In fact, all ten of the rescued pups have survived the first night. This is a huge comfort to all of us.

Week One
Loss and Survival

Bandit:

I am feeling better. It is so nice to stay warm. I don't know where I am but as long as the milk keeps coming I don't care. My sister is here with me and someone like Mom seems to be taking care of me. Mostly, I just sleep.

Beverly:

The feedings continue every two hours. I learn to sleep in my bed for the short intervals between feedings and wake to a musical alarm. But I am so tense the alarm is hardly needed.

As the pups learn to nurse, the feedings get a bit easier. The precious creatures are so small I can hold both of them in one hand while swapping the bottle between them. The brown pup finishes half a bottle during one feeding and I think this is the most either of them has consumed at one time. Their little bellies begin to expand. They move their legs and heads a lot but they are not able to walk. They roll around and crawl a bit on folded knees.

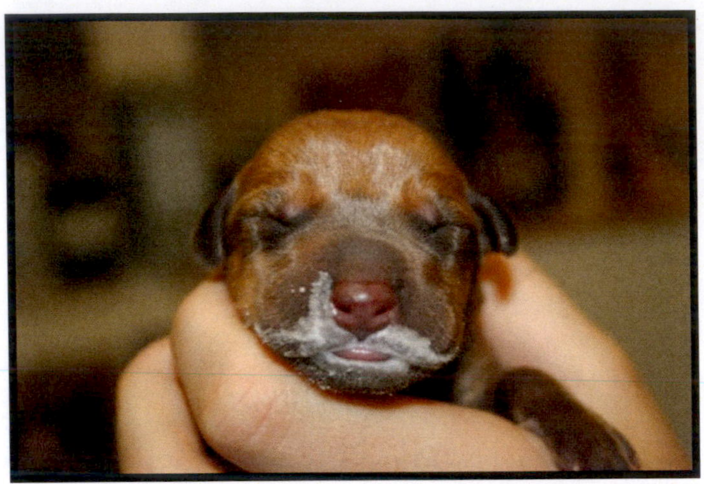

The brown pup finishes half a bottle during one feeding.

On day three I learn that one of the pups with another foster mom has died. Later that day a second one dies. An already stressful situation becomes even tenser as I worry over my babies.

Two days later I notice my pups are limp when I wake them for a feeding. Usually they wiggle and feel "alive". Now they are like rag dolls. They will not eat. Something terrible is wrong.

I call Becky at Pet Network. She tells me to use a hair blower to immediately raise their body temperature. I am also instructed to put some Karo syrup on their gums. Low temperature and low blood sugar are serious concerns that mean certain death.

About 6 p.m. I get a call to bring the puppies to the shelter immediately for a medication. The car ride seems to stimulate them a bit although they are still not very strong. They weigh in at 7 ounces each, almost double their original weight.

I see two other foster moms at the shelter with their puppies, getting medicine. We all seem tense and look like we have not slept for some time. We keep our fingers crossed.

My black and brown pups make it through another night and I am elated. But Sunday afternoon the black one fails. She is very limp and refuses to eat. I know she is dying and all I can do is wrap her in a blanket and hold her. I see some blood seeping from her mouth. She is bleeding internally and eventually dies in my arms.

I am very saddened but I cannot take time to grieve. I focus all my attention on the brown puppy.

Now that the brown pup is alone, he'll need more warmth so I add a space heater at the rear of his carrier. He rewards me by eating well.

I take him to Pet Network for assessment on Monday. Becky assures me that I am giving him the right care. Time will tell.

A concerned Pet Network staffer gives my solitary pup a teddy bear to curl up with in his carrier. I add a hot water bottle wrapped in a pink towel – poor substitutes for his lost sister.

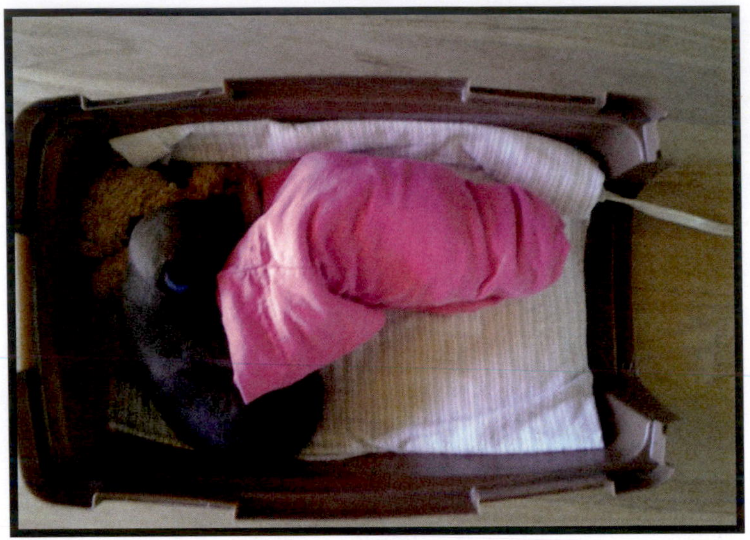

The lone pup cuddles with a teddy bear and a hot water bottle wrapped in a pink towel.

Week Two
A Closer Look

Bandit:

Things are looking up for me. I am warm and I am getting milk regularly from someone who isn't quite Mom but who is very nice to me. I am held and rubbed and I feel warm breath on my face and head. The smells around me are much better. I can crawl over soft things and burrow under them. I may be alone now but at least I feel wanted.

I still spend most of my time sleeping.

Beverly:

We've settled into a routine of feeding, belly rubbing and sleeping. Although I am still up every two hours all night, the feedings have become more routine as the puppy and I each know what to expect.

Finally I can take a moment to really examine my brown pup. He has bald spots over his eyes. I learn this is where his eyelashes will appear. His whiskers are just beginning to emerge. His umbilical cord has dried up. He is very wiggly and wants to suck my fingers. What kind of dog is he? His coloring is beginning to develop and it looks like he has a black mask across his eyes and nose. It's time to give him a name. "Bandit" comes to mind. The mask makes him look like a thief, and the little guy has stolen my heart.

Beverly examines the brown pup with the black "mask" and names him Bandit.

When I open the door of the carrier to wake and feed him, Bandit responds quickly, wobbling toward the opening. He can't hear or see yet, but perhaps he smells me or feels the jolt from the door opening. He can't stand up but he pivots and crawls on his forelegs. He is very quick. He makes small peeping sounds. I am on sensory alert. At one point I hear him and rush to his carrier to pick him up. But he is asleep. The sound was a squirrel outside the window, a false alarm.

My chest and neck are red and splotched from Bandit's sharp little nails. He squirms to crawl up my neck or into the sleeve of my kimono robe during feedings. He should be kneading and burrowing into his mother's breasts, but she is not here. At our 4 a.m. feeding, I think about his future. Wouldn't it be something if he were trained to become a rescue dog and could save someone's life? Pay it forward.

My cats are clearly annoyed at the attention Bandit is getting. They don't bother him in his carrier. But when Bandit is out crawling on his bent knees, Siena decides to investigate the wobbly brown creature. Although Bandit is growing quickly, he is still tiny compared to my cat.

Siena investigates Bandit while he crawls after a feeding. Bandit has grown but is still small compared to the cat.

I have just fed Bandit when I learn that another pup from the litter has died. A necropsy is done and samples are tested. I am called to the shelter at 7 p.m. for antibiotic medicine. This is a startling reminder that Bandit is not out of the woods. His lifeline is still a fragile one.

The veterinarian sends samples from the deceased pups to a lab to determine what they may have been exposed to in the Dumpster. The results identify several nasty bacteria. While this news dampens our optimism about saving these helpless creatures, we foster moms remain determined to succeed.

I now have antibiotics to administer to the puppy four times a day along with the feedings every two hours and a de-worming medicine. I prepare a little chart so I don't miss any important doses. Now that Bandit has a name, he is so very real and part of my life. There is no turning back. Failure is not an option.

My husband entertains little Bandit while I prepare his bottle. Although he still sleeps many hours each day, he now spends a bit of time blindly moving about exploring before and after each feeding.

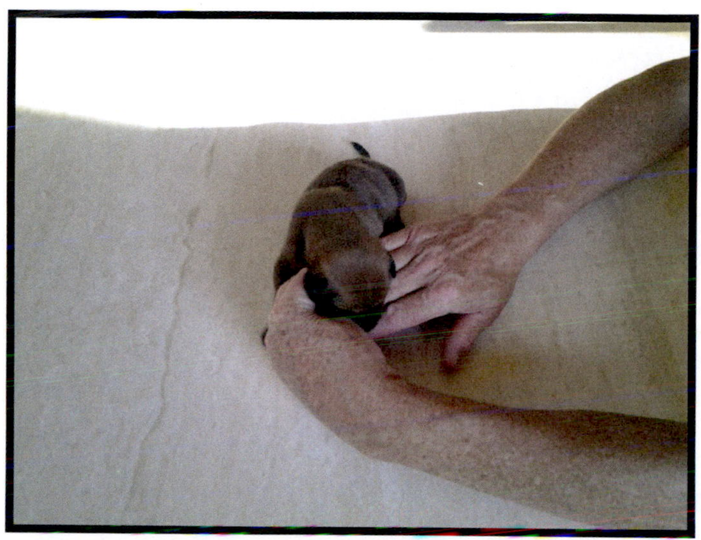

Bandit explores his surroundings even though he cannot see and cannot walk yet. He crawls on his knees.

We've just finished a bottle when I am called to Pet Network again. Channel 4 News from Reno is coming to do a story on the pups. Although we are exhausted, publicity is a good thing for the puppies and for the shelter, so we rush out. Some of Bandit's litter mates are also there and the story gets taped, edited and airs that night at 11 p.m. with anchor/reporter Elias. Bandit is a featured pup. The community is outraged that anyone could abandon the newborn pups in a Dumpster. Everyone is hoping for their survival.

At the end of week two, I have a 3-day, 2-night trip planned. It's my birthday treat and was scheduled well before Bandit arrived. It's been decades since I've given any thought to babysitters. I have to leave Bandit in foster care while we are away. Pet Network makes the arrangements. I write a long note on how my puppy likes his bottle held, where to stroke his belly, how to warm the water bottle for his carrier and fluff his bedding just so.

My husband and I enjoy our time away but I think of Bandit often. When we return home, I immediately go to pick him up. In just a few days it seems that he has grown fat and his head is larger. He seems calmer. He has a new, bigger bottle. There is so much change in only a few days, and more to come.

Week Three

All New Senses

Bandit:

What a wonderful world! I can hear sounds and I can see around me. The milk keeps coming and now I can see my bottles. I see where I want to go and I can get there pretty quickly. My mom looks wonderful to me.

I can hear myself talking. I try to tell my mom how happy I am to be here.

Beverly:

Week three is a wonderful and important week for little Bandit.

His eyes open over a two day period – first tiny slits, then half moons, then full, round and inquiring. Although the eyes look filmy for a few days, Bandit seems delighted with his new sense. When I open the door to his carrier, he comes tumbling forward with great confidence. While bottle feeding, he looks up at me and seems to stare. His eyes are deep, bright blue.

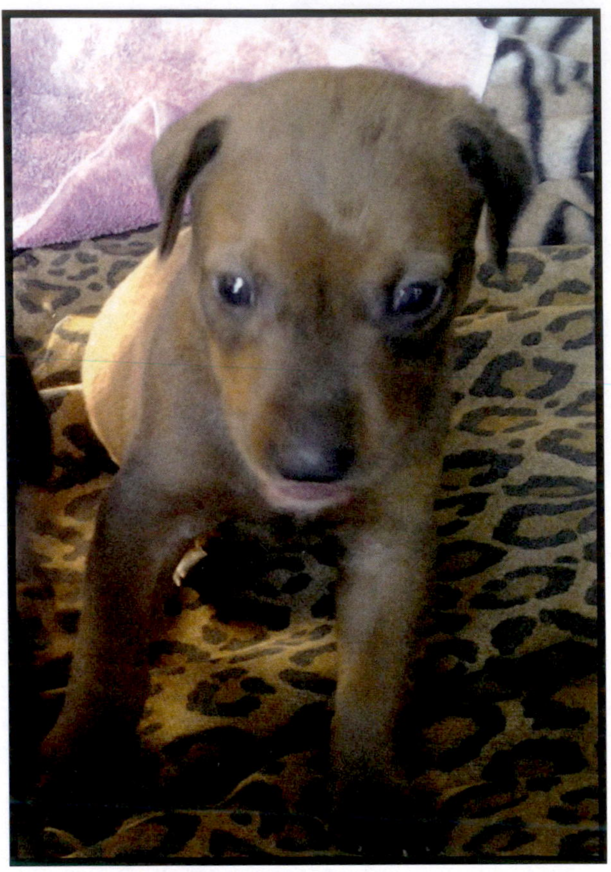

Bandit's blue eyes open and he sees his wonderful world for the first time.

Bandit's ears also become unsealed and he can hear sounds. Perhaps my quiet household isn't noisy enough for the little guy as he begins a routine of yelping loudly every so often. I think he just enjoys hearing himself. I play music for him. He seems to like the Beatles, but who doesn't?

Bandit and his remaining five littermates appear to be doing well. The biggest problem we foster moms have is getting the pups to poop regularly. Their dog mother would be licking them all over to stimulate the process. But, there is a limit to my dedication.

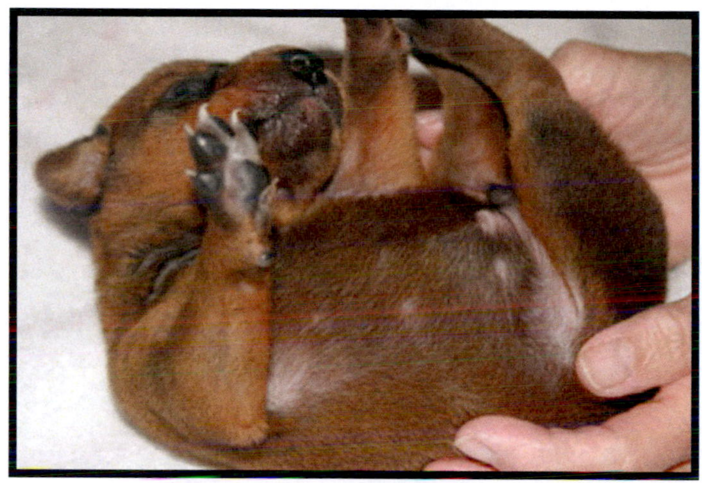

Bandit gets ready for a belly rubbing.

We are instructed to rub the pups' abdomens shortly after feedings. The desired result is achieved only some of the time. How often is enough for elimination? How much of what Bandit ingests should come out? Suddenly this most basic of body processes takes on great meaning. Bandit's belly has become so large I wonder if there is a problem. Constipation is hazardous so we get occasional expert help from the veterinarian.

Bandit routinely sleeps on his stomach or side. One morning I get up to find him lying still on his back, four legs straight up in the air. I panic, thinking I have lost him overnight. When I open the door of his carrier, he moves.

Apparently this is just one more new exploration. He shows me that he can reach the toes on his hind leg and suck them. He's limber as an acrobat.

As if seeing and hearing aren't enough new experiences, Bandit also takes his first real step this week. He is doing his usual crawling/hobbling around when suddenly he stands with his short legs fully extended and moves forward several steps. That's my boy!

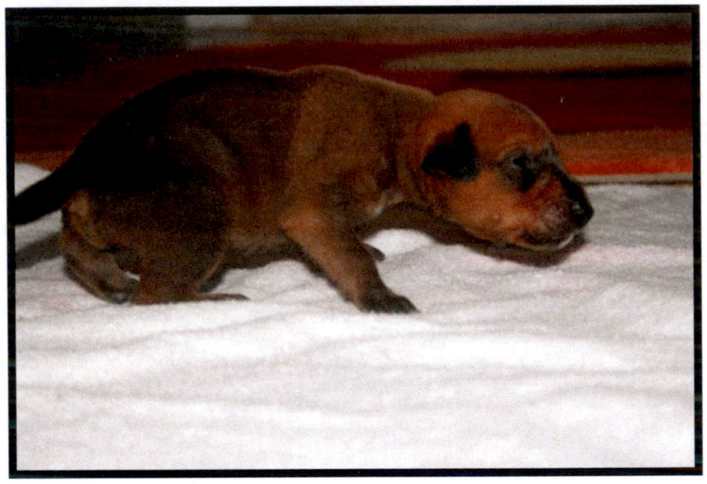

Bandit straightens his front legs and takes his first few steps.

I am still up several times during each night for bottle feedings. Bandit's demands leave almost no time for my personal agenda. While he is getting cuter each day, I am wilting.

Bandit weighed only 7 ounces in week one and he now weights over 2-1/2 pounds. He is still a one-handed bundle, but not for long. What kind of pup is he? His head seems big for his body and he has a long snout. I am worried he may be Pit Bull. That breed very unfairly has a worrisome reputation and it will be harder to find good homes for the litter of pups if they are Pits.

My friend Diane has two of Bandit's littermates. She needs to be away for a time and is very distressed about leaving her two in foster care. I know how much they mean to her so I volunteer to take them. That means I will have three bottle nursing puppies. I hope I can handle it.

Before she departs, Diane takes Bandit for two days. She has pet-friendly houseguests and the four of them enjoy caring for the pups. I wash my hair, do my nails, change the sheets, and pay the bills – all the things I have neglected since newborn Bandit took over my life.

In some ways caring for Bandit has gotten easier, or at least less stressful. We understand each other better. But caring for three 4-week old pups will be a big job.

Week Four
The Visiting Pups

Bandit:

I have some company and I am spending more time exploring outside of my carrier. It's noisy and hectic with my brother and sister here. They want to jump on me and try to get my bottle. Mom spends time with them and gives them milk. At first I don't like it so much, but then it turns out to be fun most of the time.

Beverly:

Week four is a very busy week. Two of Bandit's littermates are staying with us while my friend Diane is away. I have three carriers lined up with three needy, bottle feeding pups, all requiring periodic medications.

The additional demands are huge and the first night is a disaster for my kitchen and my family. I concentrate on organizing the process much better – formula prepared ahead, all bottles and nipples lined up, medicine syringes filled, stack of clean bedding and towels nearby, roll of paper towels and small trash bag. It helps.

The pups all cry for their formula at once. I can't stand to hear the sorrowful yelps so I open all the carriers and they tumble out, crawling onto my legs and fighting over the one nipple. I obtain a second bottle and learn to hold two bottles at a time. I wish for a third hand.

If I can get up before the pups start squealing, I may be able to awaken them sequentially. But if they awaken before me, the screams are unstoppable until all three are fed and rubbed. I am one foster mom holding two bottles trying to feed three pups. Help!

Trying to feed three puppies at a time is a challenge.

Bandit spends time with two of his littermates, Maisie and Dobbs for the first time since his rescue. He is clearly bigger and more developed than his brother and sister. He has stubby little whiskers; they have only some peach fuzz. They want to cuddle and tumble with him but he is not immediately interested. After some time together they begin to play a bit.

Littermate Dobbs jumps on Bandit's back during playtime.
He ain't heavy, he's my brother.

Good news: I am told the pups can now go for four hours between nighttime feedings. I do the math. If I can stay awake until 11:30 p.m. for a feeding, then I will have to get up only once during the night.

Bad news: No one told the pups about this change of schedule. At the 2-1/2 hour mark, I hear their persistent cries. Like a well-trained dog, I respond by delivering the milk. Reprogramming will take some time.

The three pups tumble and play a bit after each feeding. They still make peeping sounds, but once in a while I am startled by a real bark. "Peep, peep, peep, peep, **woof!**" Having the visiting pups here is very good for Bandit. Week four is an important time to begin developing social skills. It has pretty much been Bandit and me to date. Time with his littermates is important for him.

Becky at Pet Network has offered nursery day care for the Dumpster pups in the office area and I take advantage of this several days during the week. Since the pups received no antibodies from mother's milk, they shouldn't be in the shelter until they have been fully immunized, which is several weeks away. But the office folks, Becky, Jim and Annie are pitching in to provide this unique day care. I would not have been able to

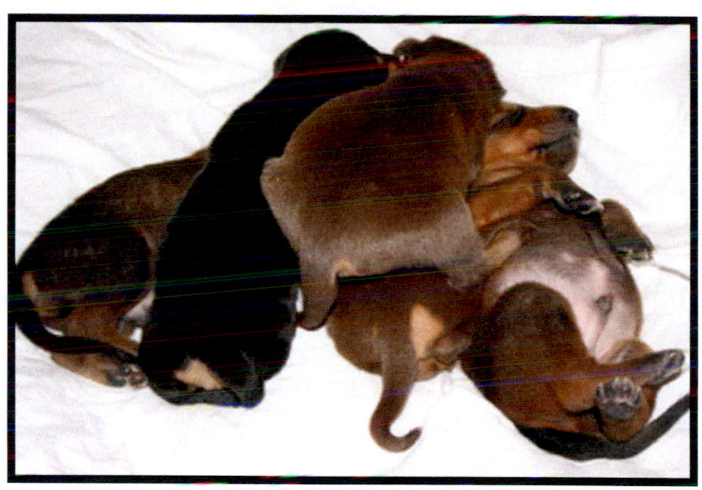

Bandit (belly up) and some littermates take a nap at nursery daycare in the Pet Network offices.

handle the responsibility of three nursing puppies without their help. So, about 9 a.m. I pack three carriers, heating pads, baby bottles, formula, clean bedding and medicine into my car. I have new found sympathy for mothers I see at airports schlepping diaper bags, bottles, blankets and strollers. The puppies receive lots of attention and special care during their outing and a baby play pen is set up to contain their enthusiasm.

No more prescribed belly rubbing! The pups are now old enough to pee and poop on their own. In fact, all three become peeing machines. It seems that every time I take them from their carriers, the bedding is wet. And when I let them out for play time, the blanket gets a soaking. I am now doing four loads of laundry a day just for the three pups. When is Diane coming back?

I learn about something called "puppy pads." The package says "absorbent, attractant." But I am not very impressed. They certainly are not the equivalent of the handy litter box for cats. The pups ignore the puppy pads and pee wherever they like.

The pups seem to be outgrowing their carriers. I improvise a "play pen" area in my rec room where they can be free to roam and sleep without the confinement of the plastic housing. It works pretty well and will contain them until they are able to climb the stone step. They respond by respecting the sleeping area and wetting only the areas outside their beds.

It's still hard to say the breed or mix of the pups, but Bandit and his friends are beginning to look like a litter of little Doberman Pinschers I saw on the Internet. I research the breed. No longer considered junk yard guard dogs, the Dobies are highly intelligent (on a par with Border Collies and Standard Poodles), very trainable, loyal to owners, friendly, made for indoor/outdoor family living. If Dobies, they will make excellent companion pets, especially with the intense human bonding they've had for their very survival.

After four weeks, we are almost half way to the time when the pups will be ready for adoption. I look back and marvel at Bandit's development and the fact we volunteers have been able to save six of ten newborn motherless creatures against incredible odds. The Dumpster pups have made the news and will certainly find loving permanent homes. There are many other wonderful dogs and cats at the shelter. They may not have had the tragic start that Bandit had, but they became homeless somewhere along the way. I hope the publicity Bandit has received will open more homes and hearts for all the homeless pets.

The visiting pups go home and Bandit and I feel relieved. It was fun to have the company, but also a lot of work and we both need a rest.

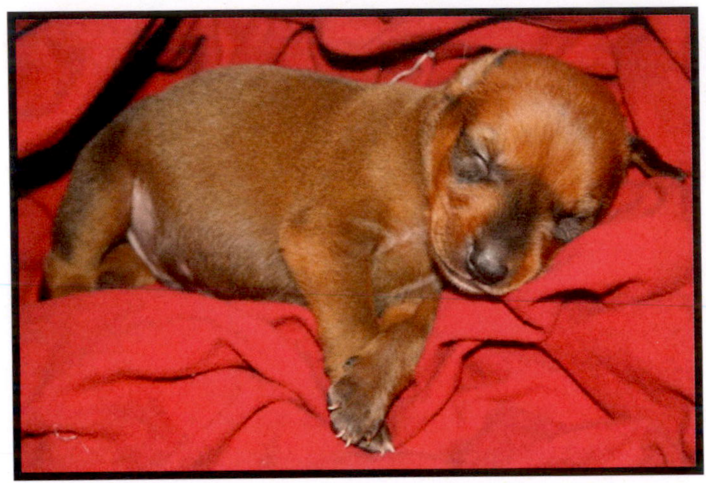

An exhausted Bandit rests after the visiting pups go home.

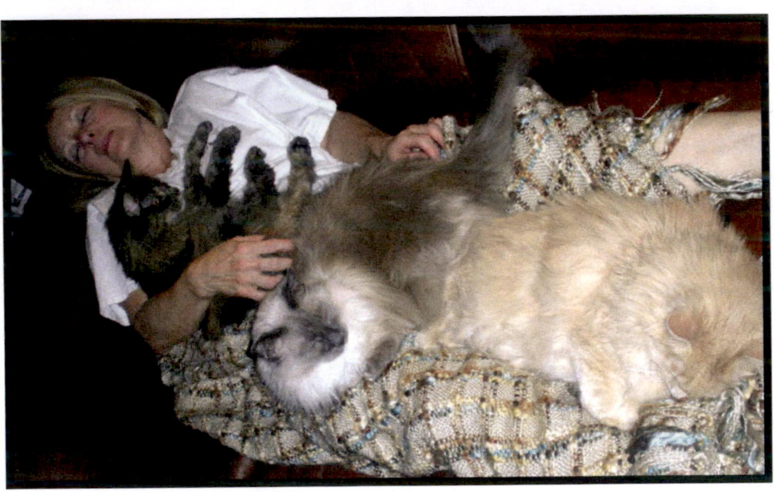

Beverly gets a cat nap as well.

Week Five

Free to Roam

Bandit:

I'm growing up; I have my own room now. I can look out the window. There are plenty of fresh towels and blankets and I am building a little fort for hiding when I sleep. There are lots of play toys and Mom visits with me in my new space often. I can't wait for her to come back.

Beverly:

Bandit begins week five by putting everything in his mouth – socks, blanket, towels, toys and newspapers. He is teething. Within a few days I see little pearly whites emerging. By the end of the week he smiles, well actually yawns, and I see a mouth full of very white teeth. With his dark blue eyes, shiny brown coat and nice white teeth, he could be a model for a dental commercial.

Bandit no longer uses his carrier. He is free to roam about the 6' x 8' pen I created for him. I leave an open carrier in his new pen but he doesn't sleep in it. Instead he takes a couple days to drag a pillow and several towels into a corner just under the overhang of a step. This is where he creates the perfect bed and sleeps most of the time.

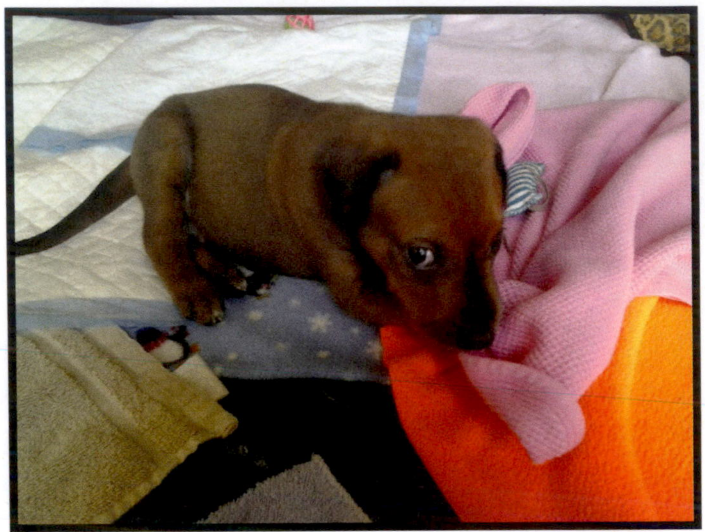

Bandit moves towels and pillows to create the perfect sleeping area in his new space.

The rest of the pen is for playing – and he does plenty of that. I try to invent puppy games that do not involve my toes or fingers. It is a challenge. I have to remember to wear socks when I visit with him. His other favorite toys are a vivid orange squeaky Sponge Bob and a striped catnip mouse that one of my kitties must have given him. I wish the kitties would join us with the games to give me a break, but they aren't yet interested in dealing with Bandit.

Here's the biggest news. Bandit eats his first actual food! It is Science Diet Gourmet Chicken from a can, mixed with some warmed weaning formula. On his very first try he devours the entire hefty portion. I thought there would be a period of weaning from the nipple, but just like that the bottle that was the lifeline binding us together is gone. My baby now eats by himself. This is the beginning of his independence. He eats this mush four times a day and we both get to sleep through the night.

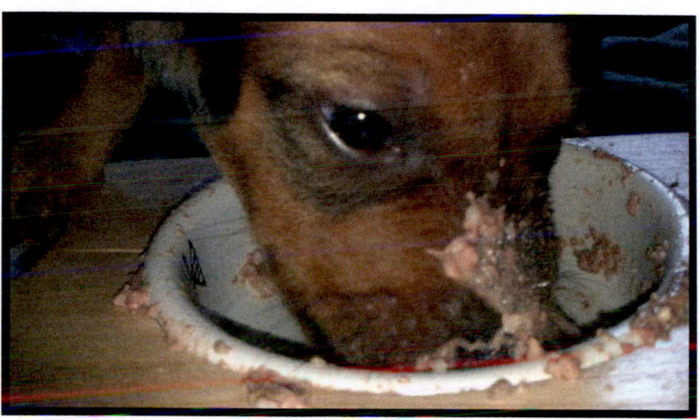

Bandit dives into his first real food, emptying the bowl and licking up all the spills.

Again we develop a routine. At feeding time, I climb into his pen with the food and formula. He jumps all over me trying to reach the ledge where I mix the gruel. When it is ready, I place the bowl on the server and he dives in. Literally, head first. He eats very quickly and noisily. Then he does a 360 degree rotation around the dish to slurp up any spills. When he can find no more spills to lick up, he comes to me and I wipe his very messy paws and face with a damp cloth. Then we settle in for a half hour of play.

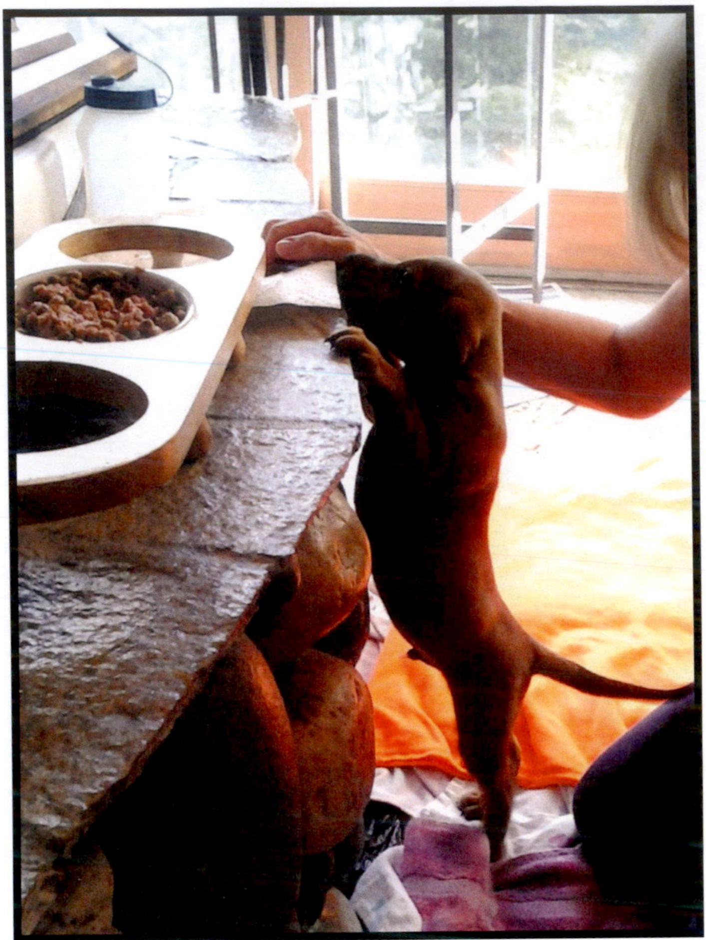

Bandit tries to reach the food before it is ready to serve. He is a very enthusiastic eater.

Bandit seems to grow before my eyes on his new diet. It is almost as dramatic as Popeye eating his spinach. I can see new muscle development is his legs and chest. He now looks like a perfect small scale model of a fully grown dog. His body has filled out to match the size of his head. He has all his parts and they are in the right proportions. Still, I cannot tell what kind of dog he is or how big he will grow. His feet do not seem oversized, a sign that he may be a modest size adult.

Now that I am Bandit's only playmate, I try to schedule some play dates for him with the pups who visited us last week. But those pups are having a setback trying to adjust to the new food. One of them requires emergency attention and they both are battling persistent diarrhea trying to adjust to the intake of protein. There could be a congenital problem with the male and I realize we are not home free yet. Again, Bandit seems larger and stronger than his littermates. I wonder if perhaps he was one of the first born and benefitted from a bit of mother's milk during the couple hours it must have taken the dog to give birth to ten babies.

So, I continue to socialize Bandit myself. I am told to touch his feet often so he will be able to withstand nail clippings. I try to get him to stop nibbling on my fingers when we play. I coach him, rather futilely, to use the newspapers for his poop. I wonder what else his mother would be showing him.

We visit Pet Network and Bandit receives his first immunization shot. I realize our time together will be coming to a close soon.

Bandit relaxes in his pen waiting for Mom to come play.

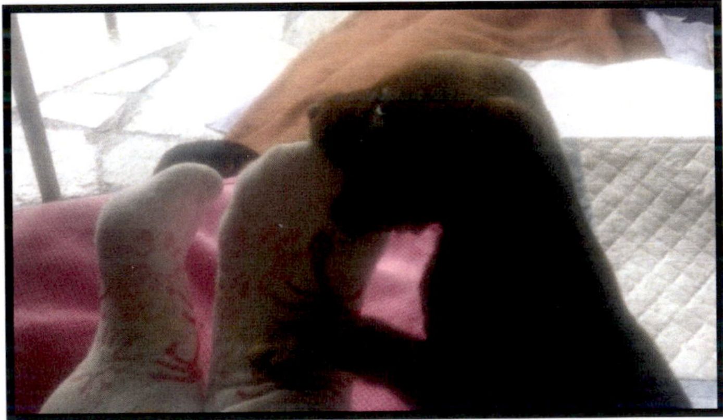

Bandit likes to play with my fingers and toes. This time I remember to wear socks!

Week Six
The Great Outdoors

Bandit:

I am eating real food and loving it. I lick my bowl clean every time. I'm not sleeping quite as much so I have more time to play. Getting toys is fun. I like crumbled papers and empty paper towel rolls too! A couple of cats keep coming by to watch me but I can't get them to come in and play yet. I'll keep talking to them.

Beverly:

Bandit's world expands dramatically during week six. His gruel is replaced by kibble mixed with some soft food. He learns to slurp water from a bowl which usually gets turned over after a few laps.

Bandit sleeps fewer hours a day now, so there is more time for play and stimulation. I invent a game of fishing using a stretchy "cat dancer." I toss out the line and eventually reel in Bandit. He fights like a marlin before I land him. We do this again and again. We also invent games with empty paper towel rolls and plastic balls.

This week I try to introduce Bandit to new people and places. I decide it is time to take him outside. My neighbors visit and four of us form a human chain to keep him from harm on his first outing. He romps around the grass delighting in the new sensations, smells and sounds. He makes his first contribution of fertilizer to the lawn and seems pleased with the deposit.

Bandit goes outside for the first time. We form a human chain around him to keep him safe.

Bandit meets two of his littermates at the Pet Network offices where we go for medication. The three energetic pups tumble together around a small room until they wear themselves out. Bandit is not the alpha male of the group, but he gets involved immediately and the others seem to like him. At one point, three of them try to squeeze into one small box. It reminds me of stuffing a Volkswagen or phone booth with too many people. He gets invited to visit the other pups in their home. This gives him more stimulation for all of his senses. But, he must conform to their house rules, which he does not like at first.

My little pup is changing appearance again. He is getting a bit taller and thinning out. His floppy ears grow longer. The vivid black mask over his eyes and nose which inspired the name "Bandit" has dissipated as he has grown and is barely evident. Who was that masked man? His most distinguishing markings now are his two-toned black and brown tail, a small white asterisk on his chest and one white toe on each back paw. He has a bit of wrinkling on his neck. His dark blue eyes are now ringed in light brown.

Bandit chases the fallen leaves on a windy day during his second time outside.

I decide to take Bandit outside again. This time it is just the two of us and not the best of days. The wind is gusting. Fallen blowing leaves attract Bandit's attention and I keep taking them from his mouth as they are covered in sap. There are far too many yellow jackets hovering and I keep redirecting the pup away from a large boulder that may contain the nest.

I am bending and stooping constantly to keep up with him. Suddenly I hear a sorrowful whimper. He looks up with surprised and sad eyes and limps to me on three legs. I pick him up and he licks a back foot. He has been bitten by one of the yellow striped pests.

I immediately call Becky at Pet Network but do not reach her. I get online looking for facts. After several reliable sources concur, I realize that as long as he is not one of a very small percentage of creatures that will have a severe allergic reaction, it isn't much to worry about. I watch him closely for over an hour and he seems dejected but not physically worse for the wear. We move inside and rather than continue to play he mopes over to his sleeping area and buries his head in the blanket.

It seems that Bandit is a bit over-dramatic about his wound. It makes me realize just how protected he has been. Yes, he had a very ignoble start in the Dumpster and probably deserves his fair share of coddling. But in truth he has been living in a climate controlled bubble for the past six weeks. He gets warm, clean bedding twice a day; four warm meals lovingly prepared and served on schedule; great background music; my company on command; dog toys and cat toys and homemade play things; nail clipping pedicures every other week; and he can watch as much television as he wishes! He has gone from being discarded and unwanted to being spoiled and adored.

I am thinking Bandit needs to get real – start learning what life is really like. Just as I plan ways to introduce him to a less self-centered world, my cat Rowdy comes over and swats him on the head. I guess this will be a family project.

Weeks Seven and Eight
Breaking Out, Saying Goodbye

Bandit:

I see Mom coming down stairs to feed me and going back upstairs after we play. I want to get to those stairs and surprise her. But I can't climb over the barrier around my room. I keep trying but when I knock something out of the way, she keeps putting it back. Even though I can't get to the stairs, Mom picks me up and takes me upstairs and outside. There are so many smells and sounds. I can't explore quickly enough.

Beverly:

Bandit continues his growth spurt during weeks seven and eight. He is now 10 pounds and pretty strong. He is bigger than my smallest cat, Whisper. But he has a way to go before he overtakes the others. He no longer bites my fingers. His mouth is bigger now so he latches onto my whole forearm instead!

Bandit almost reaches the ledge where I scoop his food. Becky at Pet Network tells me she sees his ribs and I should increase the amount of food I serve him. He is very happy to hear that!

The pup is finally tall enough to make it up the two steps that have been separating him from his next adventure. But it takes two more days before he is brave enough to make the plunge going down the steps by himself.

One evening, Bandit breaks through the barrier that I have been building higher and higher each week to contain him in the puppy zone of my house. I give up. He now has increased his territory to the whole lower level.

Bandit breaks out of his puppy zone space and runs into Rowdy the cat.

We visit Pet Network and Bandit receives a collar, harness and leash. The collar and leash are printed with orange flames a la biker chic. But they look great against his warm brown fur. Now we are ready for walks.

After two failed attempts, I get the harness on correctly. I attach the leash, and then pack a plastic doggie waste bag and some water. My husband insists I take the bear repellent also as Bandit may look like a tasty morsel to some of the wildlife up here. After considerable preparedness, we are finally ready and off we go. We make it to the end of the driveway and Bandit is ready to go back into the garage.

But the next day we try this again and we are real walkers. We go down the road and around the corner, sniffing and prancing (him, not me.) We meet a few people who recognize him as the Dumpster Pup from the local newspaper articles. They gush over him and he gives them his best poses.

We learn Bandit loves grass, doesn't mind pine needles and dry dirt, could do without the drain grates at the edge of the road and turns out to be a pretty good rock climber. The plentiful bird and squirrel noises are of great interest. He is also intrigued by a silver tarp covering a neighbor's wood pile.

We finish our walk, go back inside the house, and he poops! I guess he prefers dirtying my floor to soiling the great outdoors. Luckily I still have the doggie waste bag in my pocket!

The truth is that Bandit has outgrown me. When his needs were basic I responded instinctually. Although I had no experience with dogs at all, keeping him warm, dry, nourished and loved came naturally. Now that he has matured, I am in over my head. He is ready to learn how to do the things dogs should do: poop and pee in the right places; lift one leg while peeing; respond to commands like sit, heel, fetch; lick his private parts in public; and, hang his head out the car window. He needs a proper coach.

Bandit explores during his first walk on a leash.

Bandit also needs more space. I notice that he is less interested in my flesh when we are outside or in new environments. My house is not puppy-proof. It is time to turn him back to Pet Network. I love the little guy, but as my friend observes, I love him best when he behaves like a cat.

Each day I decide I am ready to let him go. Then he wins another 24 hours by showing unabashed excitement when he sees me and tilting his head just so. I adore him. They call it puppy love. But if you love him, let him go.

We spend our last evening together. We take a long walk, dine and play. I consider letting him sleep on the bed or in the bedroom until my husband and two of my cats object loudly. I pack the pup's special things and prepare for his morning departure. Bandit will leave my home but he will stay in my heart always.

In the morning we have a final walk, and then head to Pet Network. It takes three trips into the shelter to deliver Bandit, his food, his carrier and all the special toys and bedding he has accumulated in eight weeks. Although I am positive this is the right thing to do, I start sobbing. Leaving him is easier said than done.

Bandit will be neutered at Pet Network and become available for adoption. Between 3 and 4 million healthy unwanted dogs and cats are euthanized in the U.S. each year. Bandit is safe. And neither Bandit nor his littermates will ever create another unwanted litter.

On July 23rd, I responded to an emergency and took Bandit and a littermate home. They were only hours old. I had hoped to keep them alive overnight until experienced help became available. Eight weeks later, I have taken Bandit from a 4-ounce trembling neonate to a 10-pound healthy young pup. It was an experience I will never forget. He is now ready to enrich the lives of a devoted new family.

Weeks Nine and Ten

Reunion and Adoption

Beverly:

Bandit and the other surviving Dumpster pups are reunited at Pet Network where they quickly garner widespread attention from visitors and staff. The animal care employees have their hands full!

Pet Network's Melissa holds Maisie and Dobbs, the pups who stayed with us during week four, and Bandit on the right.

Pet Network's Jess holds Diva (aka Maggie), Otter and Reggie.

The pups are pronounced healthy by the veterinarian and their spay/neuter surgeries are scheduled. The pups are an interesting array of blue, brown and black colorings. What kind of dogs are they and how big will they grow? Saliva from the pups is sent to a DNA lab in order to determine the breed.

Pet Network holds a very lively coming out party for the puppies and almost 100 people from the community come to the shelter to meet the famous creatures. All the pups are friendly, playful and well behaved, showing how much they have bonded with people and each other during their fostering experiences. Becky announces at the party that the DNA lab determined the puppies are a Doberman and Border Collie mix. Those are two very smart breeds.

The Dumpster pups are reunited at Pet Network. Bandit is 3rd from the right.

My friend Rich Chew captures this amazing photo of all six Dumpster pups on a couch in the shelter.

The six surviving Dumpster pups pose together. Bandit is being squeezed on the far right. They are ten weeks old.

The adoption process begins and applications from local residents are given priority. Each pup is matched with a permanent home. Bandit gets adopted by an active couple who will take him hiking and cross country skiing and kayaking and give him the training he needs to become one very special and lucky dog.

Bandit's new owners are generous souls who share photos and videos of their pup's continuing development with me. They arrange play dates at the beach with some of Bandit's littermates. Some of the Dumpster pups attend doggie day care at Pet Network from time to time. I have visited with Bandit there and he seems delighted to see me – all 45 pounds of him. But to be honest, he seems delighted to see everyone. He is enthusiastic but well-mannered and very handsome. I think I did okay raising my first puppy!

Bandit:

Like I said, I am one lucky dog.

At ten weeks old and ten pounds of energy,
Bandit is ready for adoption.

ADOPTION DAY!

Bandit poses with his new family (above) and thanks Melanie for picking him out from all the rest!

Bandit is now living the life of a lucky dog at beautiful Lake Tahoe with his adoptive forever family.

.

Rob and Bandit enjoy kayaking

Melanie and Bandit play on the beach.

Bandit experiences his first snow in his new winter jacket.

Made in the USA
Monee, IL
28 April 2024

57598103R10038